WHAT THIS BOOK IS ABOUT

A TRUE STORY....

… it's a bit mysterious – thrilling in parts, and it concerns *something* you really should know.

I don't know who or what you are, or why you have landed here. But as you're here now let's quickly explore & analyse a stragegic aspect of our so-called Space-Age.

It involves Modern architecture – <u>the design of landing craft / Modules</u>, and a vital **MISSING product range** nobody mentions!

Discover the beneficial, endless possibilities by producing those!

Could that *CORRECTIVE ACTION* help people, and get us back on track, on this planet?

PROJECT: *it*

HASSLE-*FREE Living!*

By Jillionsing

CONTENTS

INTRODUCTION

I wish it wasn't such a long story.

I feel as if I've been wandering in a wilderness (for longer than Moses).

Early on, I was bewildered. I knew I was not wanted - my parents rejected me because they didn't want a girl that looks mixed-race. I didn't understand them. My dad - a workaholic that drank too much. My "mother" mocked and beat me... When I asked "why am I treated differently?" she said "because you're special." *Uh?* By age 8, with nobody to talk to, I stopped talking...

By about age 11, I felt a deep sense of sadness and shame that still persists (brought on by what happened in Biafra – the mass starvation – haunting images of skeletal women sitting in barren fields – on the cracked ground, stroking their infants – no milk - severe drought, no energy to walk any further – looking so sad as they waited to die. I could not believe nobody was rushing to help them! What must they have thought about us!? I just couldn't get over it. **<u>So much AWFUL SUFFERING in this world!</u>** I felt distanced from those that laughed at me and called me "Thingy" when I reminded them about Biafra, and I was told: "Don't let it affect you."

At roughly the same time I lost my family (after having very tearful nightmares predicting that was going to happen). I didn't have a clue about what was happening to me. "Life" was very much like trying to see in a mist...

"SOMETHING MUST DONE..."

That despondency grew into a **deep** *YEARNING*, until I was conciously aware the same thoughts were repeating in my mind - I was hoping so much for... *something*, I was actually silently praying... and looking for... *something* I couldn't have described. I'm sure I didn't know the words to express it, but it was as if I was thinking: *There's got to be a better way than this! Something! Easier. EFFICIENT! What is it? What could it be? I've got to find it...*

Then I was homeless - age 12 when first told to "**GET OUT!**" and "... and stay in the gutter where you belong." I hid in the library, and phone box... Age 17, I was accused of "... getting yourself pregnant..." and thrown out, with no money, help or support...

For 15 years I was a Homeless single parent unable to get social housing. I worked making clothes whenever I could. I've never slept on the streets (I wouldn't have survived if I had). I've never used alcohol, or done drugs, crime or prostitution. I wasn't lazy, a hell raiser, or a problem to live with. I was just always having to move to try to find somewhere decent so we could live in peace, and prosper. After move No. 263, I stopped counting...

Age 30, on my last legs... I started having *VISIONS...* (I wasn't *delirious?* but I was dying of starvation and exhaustion...) and I saw pictures / very clear images (in my mind) of a time in the future – a new way of life – how life could be!

Even when I was able to define the elusive *"something"* 'it' still had no real form! So it's still like an unsolved riddle! Yes, it keeps me on my toes, doesn't let me sleep long, makes my head buzz, and ears ring (with pressure) (but it hasn't made my chest roar yet).

I know I am not unique. Too many people are suffering a much harder "life"... It affects many different people who are finding "life" really difficult... ... I must have heard at least 500 people exasperately say **"... something must done about it..."**

"... it's BEEN A LONG TIME COMING..."

I'm still not sure about this! Could *'it'* be a *"calling"*?
My task / role (*predestined? mission?*):
<u>SAFELY DELIVER *it*</u> to capable hands.
(Does that mean - find a suitable manufacturer?)

<u>PLEASE FORGIVE ME</u>. I am very **SORRY** *'it'* is **OVERDUE**.
I tried to make *'it'* happen - I did all I could. To the best of my
ability. I gave *'it'* all I could. But I **<u>FAILED</u>**.
I know self- control matters, but **WAH!**

35 YEARS later (Age 67):

"To get it out of your system, PUT PEN TO PAPER!"

That's what I'm doing... Because I worry about what could
happen should clear thinking diminish...

... **TIME IS RUNNING OUT** - *'it'* is still trapped inside me! I
don't want *'it'* to die (when I do). So, I now feel like Beethoven.
I need to do what I just must, to get 'it' out of me.

I've been isolated from the business world for a very long
time, and I don't mind about that. Same as with my parents
their religion is money. I'm not a "God-botherer" but from
where I see it, avarice should not rule! I'm not doing this to

make money – *'it'* is really not about that! I only feel the urge to boost them because whilst *'it'* is eluding... nobody can get on track.

I have never desired fame or fortune. I like being a Hermit with only a very few knowing only a little about me. I've never had "a social life." And that is how I want to stay.

CHAPTER 1

LET'S GET TO *it*

1979 – 1983

I was a very poorly paid, self-taught, confidence-lacking, working-class / backstreet fashion **DESIGNER** specialising in **new product TREND-FORECASTING**.

(I had too many clients and a fledgling studio in London. All my money had been spent turning a couple of derelict, damp basement rooms into a place where a small team could work. I slept there with my 10 year old child at night. Then exhaustion, chronic back pain from an injury, and an unaffordable rent hike forced me to throw in the towel – we had to go through the rigmarol of being homeless again).

1988

I got the idea for *it* (when I was still homeless). Then I some-how sensed my father (location unknown to me) had just

1

died... A voice in my head (my father's?) instructed me to draw what I had pictured in my head. I grumbled "I can't draw buildings," then deciding I'd love to live in a cottage (but without **the usual problems - damp, crumbling, hard to heat, in wrong location, rot...**) I drew a picture... a rather strange looking *entity?* appeared on my tatty drawing board - *something very different* had... *come out!*

I looked at 'it' and 'it' looked at me...

Thereafter, inseparable – *it,* and me with a Module in my mind's eye!

UK: 1989

I copyrighted **Project:** *it...* when the need for **"<u>AFFORDABLE HOMES</u>"** was taking off. ...Having been Homeless, I thought everybody understood the Homeless need to have a *HOME* – that it was unnecessary to explain that, or justify why *it* is needed (as that is as clear as ice). What transpired made me realise there was no political will to change the status quo.

Mrs Thatcher's **<u>dreadful</u> "GREED** is Good" **poisoning**...

So many of the Homeless - starving and freezing - desperately packed into "Cardboard Cities" - even under the Queen Elizabeth Hall...

Most popular phrase? **"Go for it."** Nobody specifying what *it* is!

"The **BIG ISSUE**" magazine launched, raising awareness and money for Homeless street vendors...

Toshiba's "Year of Invention" Competition (I could not enter as I was not under-25).

Prince Charles's campaign to persuade the world his personal preference for traditional architecture is right to be favoured (to turn people away from all that is Modern?) The Architects debated - **"leaving it out!"** *(Yes, "God is in the details").*

When I approached a few British industrailists hoping to enlist their support for *it,* I was given the run around. ICI said "try Shell." Shell said "try ICI." I was finally thwarted by Shell UK when Mr. Newman in New Materials said: **"It's not something we can invest in. There is no market for it, so no money is in it for us."**

A meeting with my hero ("the design guru" / founder of **HABITAT,** Sir Terence Conran) did not go how I wanted. He didn't give me a chance to say a word about *it.* He waffled on about his dream to put the homeless in his discarded wooden packing cases... When I knew he wasn't going to champion *it,* I'm ashamed to say I fell asleep in his office - in the middle of the afternoon.

I got the impression during those meetings (and others) this idea was **not new** to them – for them it is something that goes round and round - like a fly dying - it's "a source of great amusment" that it never gets anywhere!

Then a "friend" snapped at me: "Don't waste your money on it! **HUMANITY IS NOT WORTH SAVING.**"

I couldn't think of a retort to that! My faith in Humanity back then was not something I was sure about.

Oh dear, I was hoping to find a company with some enthusiam. But there's nobody in my life who's eyes do not drift off in boredom if I mention 'it' during a conversation. That has put me off talking about *it*.

Without backing, or a plan (just stubbornly refusing to accept toxic **condemning** of the *whole?* world!) I started **RESEARCHING** *it* to find out what other people / experts know about *it*. I didn't know what else I could do! I wanted to find out everything I possibly could about *it,* whilst hoping to ascertain if there is a way to make it acceptable to upper echelons.

Every day I expected to stumble on at least one insurmountable **FACT** that means *it* is impossible to do. (If that had happened I would have accepted that as the time for me to give it up).

I found there is a good answer to overcome every stumbling block...

TRACKING AND ANALYSING DISASTERS as they were happening around the world (from a safe distance) was shocking - a steep, **EDUCATIVE** learning curve for me that taught me a great deal.

"WHY IS NOBODY HELPING US?
WE NEED HELP NOW!"

Upset by events, and not able to help those survivors, I somehow managed to keep working on this (unpaid, altruistic) project, always asking myself:

WOULD IT HELP if it was there for them now?

I just knew *it would make all the difference*.

That process also taught me, the actual **MARKET SIZE** for it is considerably larger than I realised.

(To research I followed relevant news reports wherever the media were focusing on in the world... I collected **QUOTES** – including phrases / sentences using the word 'it' - for, or against it, that struck me as **SIGNIFICANT...**

Doing that was a task and a half – I only had a small black & white TV, no PC's back then... I filled piles of journo pads with notes speedily scribbled... I put all that information into categories with chronological lists...

Because I believe _it's recent history_ matters, later on, I used a computer to make that into a Non-fiction reference book...)

2004 (After researching this full-time since 1989):

By making a careful record of what I found out, I ended up with **INDISPUTABLE EVIDENCE,** to establish _it is_ FEASIBLE. **PROOF!** That _it is_ **DOABLE.**

(I usually hid my experimental drawings in a drawer due to anxiety / self-doubt as soon as they were finished. Then I'd forget about them). I never had those doubts about _it._ Reassuringly, my respect for _it_ grew **STRONGER** as my knowledge expanded - _its appeal_ only intensified, consolidating _it_ firmly in my mind. Truthfully, _it_ has never failed to _FASCINATE_ me.

(Sticking with a design for so long is also unusual for me because my mind bounced around quite a lot. I think that's because I miss the old days when I was with like-minded creative souls _"Think-Tanking."_ "We're not allowed to use that phrase now." Really!? _Oh, for heaven's sake!)_

I contacted publishers (again), and got nowhere.

2007

I tried hard to complete this project... I still dreamt all the time about getting *it off the ground...*

I got a website and with no advertising offered my book as a free pdf download (just before ebooks became popular). My forum was going well. In a couple of months, 33,000 visitors signed the guest book... Then I got hacked out of admin – the forum was taken over and ruined by spammers. I had to close tthe website down.

I'd paid to have a shortened book printed, advertising my website. I was so disappointed I couldn't even market that! I gave 50 copies to an Oxfam shop, the remaining 50 are still in the box.

HELL broke out in "my life" (again)... "Life" was still intent on stopping me succeeding. I could only **WAIT** - put *it* on the backburner (again), and hope other people will *get it together...*

NEGLECTED BY "THE BIG-BOYS / MONEY MEN"

Just in case this *kind* of design - *it* - still fails to appear, so *its potential* is not **LOST** - to protect and SAVE *it,* for 'insurance,' I stored a digital copy of my research – sadly consigning *it* to gather cyber dust, telling myself that's the best I can do.

2011

A real-life **DEMON** (from my childhood) was still out in force to get me... (Again), I didn't believe I would survive... I was told: "You have to fight!" about 5 times... (Not fisty-cuffs! I mean mentally and physically - exerting as much effort as can be mustered). Hard, when you've lost the will (again) to live... Then, I had to jump many high hurdles just to stay alive... (I think I only survived because I had some help from above).

DISTRACTIONS: Other people's problems, mundane chores etc., used up the time I wanted to devote to *it*. More years went by - my patience very sorely tested – until... my body just took over! Hello, what's this about? (uncontrollable?) shaking! I was in a dither, quivering! (My childhood illness was back). Only way to resolve? **AVOID** other people!

2020

Incredible! I never thought I'd *outlive* a **powerful force** deliberately causing **BAD - REALLY HEAVY TIMES!** Even my head is free'd of those demons now - it's free'ing just to know there *is* an end to woes!

(Bane of my existence now? After such a long journey I am tired of **drab leaky houses**. To get a home, I had to repair 5 wrecks doing the donkey work, "living" in dusty building sites. Now, looking out, I can't see one TREE. That

makes me want to cry. Like many people I suffer inadequate heating, condensation, black mould growth, crumbling, cracked walls requiring never-ending patching and
painting, no Recycling store run by the Community, heavy
traffic, **fumes**, too many cars, nowhere to park - even for
the disabled, smarmy local government, distant and unac-
countable "local" MP's...

Ooh! Brain freeze! What was I going to say? My teeth are
chattering and my hands and feet are so cold! I thought
the weather forecast said it's getting warmer – **it doesn't**
feel *like it!* I can't remember where I was going with this
now! *Quickly! Change the Subject!* Yes, we've got to love
it. Oh! *its just come back to me.* Sorry! My memory - I'm
really not *with it!*)

Sadly, *it* <u>**IS STILL NOT AN AVAILABLE OPTION**</u> - the
LACK of *truly* **low-cost housing** *is an issue* that **still hasn't
been sorted out!**

CONFUSION IS STILL HALTING PROGRESS! And I still
don't know what to do about *it.* **NIGHTMARE!** I still can't find
a publisher because my book is too big!? I can't have a book
about it that's as **heavy as a brick**!

I just can't accept this <u>*REMEDY* that is needed so much,</u> seems
likely to be **MISUNDERSTOOD & FORGOTTEN** forever,
because *it* was <u>**wrongly**</u> bypassed / dismissed in the past...

And my poor frazzled brain still can't believe - instead of *just getting on and doing it* - after so many fruitless years of hoping and just expecting to see *it up-and-running* - my role could still be I have to explain *it!*

Me, on a podium? Uh-Oh! Very **SCAREY!** That is never going to happen. I'm not a public speaker! What if I do *it* an **INJUSTICE**? My battered looks are enough to put people off. **ARGH!** Curses! My research is not common knowledge and I can't even quickly flip to a printed page in my book to find a good quote to rebuke... Given those prospects *it* doesn't stand a chance! I am not happy.

There are 100's and 1,000's of eloquent, academically qualified, experienced people much more likely to do an excellent job of standing up for *it*.

(H'mm. And some professionals / "experts" - **"paid mouthpieces"** are often used for dark pleasure, to **DISCREDIT** *the truth*).

WHO could I ask to explain *it* for me? Even the media only mention the word "modular" rarely - *it's* **a joke!** (Yes, *"it is hidden in the long, long grass..."*)

NOBODY IS SPEAKING OUT about *it!* (I did hear one lady MP approx. 3 years ago trying to tell Parliament about some "exciting modular successes" in north UK. Other MP's weren't listening - they drowned out her voice with their usual raucous jinking...)

I am only one **IMMENSELY FRUSTRATED DESIGNER...** Surely there are others? Maybe makers of other types of Modular structures are willing to speak up?

HELL! I have just heard the "news."

Downing Street has recently **GIVEN PERMISSION** for new **MODULAR NUCLEAR POWER STATIONS** to be built!.

Terrible Transgressions! They are getting *it* **Wrong! BIG- time! RADIOACTIVE... ALL DANGERS IGNORED!** My blood recoils, I feel cold with **HORROR.**

WHY do we have such a **CRUEL,** crazy, complex world today, with the **State allowing TERRIFYING Things** whilst inexplicably **BLOCKING** *the Truly Beneficial... ??*

I don't get it.

QUEST FOR GREATER TRANSPARENCY!

I now feel resolutely **COMPELLED** to bring *it* to the fore in peo- ple's minds. What matters most is the majority of people are

AWARE of _its existence_ (so _it's_ not entirely in the hands of only a very few who **don't** care about any of this). I just need to get the idea across! _Spread the word!_ Get _it_ <u>**OUT THERE**</u> – known as a <u>**VIABLE**</u> possibility, even if _it_ only "widens the debate."

But that means me (of all people!) writing a book? That is the only hope I've got realistically to be able to change anything.

My **MANTRA** now? _There's got to be a way! It's like having a baby! One final push..._

"BETTER LATE, THAN NEVER"

Ooh I'm struggling! I'm sorry I'm not explaining this well! I'm not a trained author! I expect I will mostly get **PUT DOWNS:** "You don't know what you're talking about..." "You're a past-it, pathetic inventor."

Oh crap! They still want to **KILL** "to make a living"!?

<u>I do not want to take anybody on</u>!

I am not saying I have got everything 100% correct!

I just want _it TO BE DONE, PROPERLY AND WELL!_

I'm not an illustrator! If my child'ish drawings (of *it*) make you look at *it* twice, and you produce better, I think that's *GREAT.*

My biggest **FEAR**? What if my inadequacies mean this message **FAILS** to reach **POLICY MAKERS?** All those in charge, so they **don't** open their eyes to the <u>sad fact</u> their decisions *are* taking us in the **WRONG** direction?

"NOTHING VENTURED, NOTHING GAINED"

How much easier "life" would be if a <u>HOTLINE</u> *(some Communication!)* was open for **"GOOD IDEAS people"** to call the President, Prime minister, or newspaper. Wouldn't that save a lot of **Headaches?**

"Barnes Wallis here. I know how to fix this problem that's perplexing you. I've invented a Bouncing bomb, to stop the infernal Jerries..."

"Civil" "servant" (in no uncertain terms): **"GET LOST."**

YIKES! Wars wont be won with that attitude!

20 December 2021

News report: "... The UK Conservative government said <u>they do not know how to 'LEVEL UP'</u> - <u>it is a puzzle they have not yet found the answer to</u>..."
followed by: Boris Johnson's speech bigging up his party in Parliament:
"… and we are giving **£MILLIONS** to local councils who can best decide what to do with it..."

THAT IS UNBELIEVABLE?

Oh dear. Homeless citizens have, for **YEARS,** collasped and been found **frozen to death** outside council offices...

Local Authorities don't **MISSPEND?** Ask NHS staff who must surely be sick of having so many people **uncivily dumped** (to be lost?) in the Health service, by councils eagerly **EVADING** their <u>**DUTY OF CARE!**</u>

The British government confessed to **IGNORANCE**, to **DENY** a fairly *obvious way forward*, so the powers-that-be <u>can get away with yet **MORE DELAY**/s **(after** forcing the public to<u> **WAIT 2 decades**</u> for wealth to "trickle down")!

As *it is* OBVIOUS to a non-academic person such as me, how can they (capitalist bureaucrats), with all their con-tacts / **TOP** connections - **not** be aware, or informed?

14

<u>WHAT IF</u> they really **DON'T KNOW** *HOW TO DO it?*

<u>Does that mean they might be interested in finding out</u>?

(How to classify the type of well-paid ministers that **DON'T** care about understanding or relieving other people's suffering? Are they upholding policy? Or have they gone rogue? In which case, why don't we simply get them to sign a contract when taking office that terminates if they are in breach?)

<u>Governments have had a very long time to *work it out!*</u>

<u>Churchill's **PREFABS**</u> were a success story...

(Such a pity the fabric of those **"<u>VERY POPULAR</u>"** homes rotted after approx. 40 years...)

Has Whitehall been aware of the *ADVANTAGES* **<u>FOR</u>** **<u>CITIZENS</u>** - if they had Modules (or equivalent) to live in - for many years?

Are a **COVERT** group of **VULTURES sitting on** *it* (and using every dirty trick) (to cling onto power, to extract **HEAVY TAXES** - for spending / **MISAPPROPIATION** with **<u>no</u> <u>close</u> <u>scrutiny</u>?)

(I don't know. That's not for me to decide. Yes, I would like to hear Inquiries by Select Committees...)

The **TRAVESTY** of this situation reminds me of a story about **HITLER**

(Sorry! This is not a **NEGATIVE** irrelevancy. It concerns a *POSITIVE ENERGISING OPTION* we still have, to help alleviate problems):

... When the ports were blocked and civilians were starving... Hitler gave money to industrialists telling them to *come up with Alternatives* to **MATERIALS IN SHORT SUPPLY** (that was called the Ersatz Scheme). One of the new materials invented was a very early form of plastic.

HITLER CHOSE WAR (Against the world) rather than *invest in those NEW MATERIALS*. That was Hitler's choice. Hitler opted to not help people. Hitler turned his back on *all the good things* he could have achieved... (That new material was used to house the 1st radio...)

Maybe Downing Street is so preoccupied with the Taliban, for example - still seeking a way out of the **MESS** in Afghanistan, and other countries, they still haven't had time to *give it another thought*?

Yes, it does matter how much thought you put into it!

Are leaders bothered when **HISTORY REPEATS?** Or do they only gleefully rub their hands for the **SPOILS** enjoying the **FALL-OUT** as entertainment?

SOBERING

Too many <u>**ALCOHOL IMPAIRED**</u> decisions are taken, and too much **COCAINE** is up the noses of **delirious weaponised** men **IMMORALLY kontrolling** Citizens - **extremely badly** - whilst **madly** refusing to accept they are not God, but mortal beings *highly-likely* to experience an admonishing <u>**PUNISHMENT**</u> when they die and encounter <u>*THE TRUTH*</u>.

HUMBLING

Making things requires practice and skill/s. I can't make a butterfly – that is impossible (recreating *exquisite beauty,* every fine detail *nature* bestows, *giving it life* so it flies effortlessly).

So, when <u>**some people refuse**</u> to *<u>believe there is anything</u> <u>GREATER</u>* than **<u>Man,</u>** that irritates me.

Surely that *ALMIGHTY DIVINE PRESENCE* is clearly evident. LOOK at what that has *IMMORTALLY, PROLIFICALLY ORIGINATED AND PRODUCED.*

<u>That is valid **proof** a *HIGHER INTELLIGENCE* exists.</u>

So, why not simply **<u>RESPECT</u>** that?

(When I learnt and accepted that *TRUTH*, I was at *PEACE* - happy to be *freely GUIDED* by that *STRONG SPIRIT*. That is why I am *DEDICATED,* to *OUR CREATOR,* and trust *that).*

(I hear you arguing! But cloning is **Copying**. Man's plan to clone to "prevent **THE EXTINCTION OF EVERY SPECIES**" due to **MAN'S DESTRUCTION** is so far removed - that in no way can be compared to *FAITHFUL AND LOVING PRINCIPLES*).

VERY <u>CRUCIAL</u> TIME!

"LOOSE TALK COSTS LIVES"

The reason Kontrollers use heavy force is they know we wouldn't vote for it? Now do you begin to grasp how **CONFUSION** arises, especially when politicians (actors) make many promises and assertions using the word "it" to mean many different things, slyly saying what they think we want to hear... They spin it out. We, the people, get nowhere!

Humanity / **VOTERS ARE DECIDING**

Do we want leaders continuing to "act" with **cold indiffer- ent arrogance** towards us - whilst politicians are, <u>at our</u>

expense, and without asking us, authoritatively leading us underdemocratically - and very **VAGUELY -** to go to **only they know where** – on a mystery ride (to a: Black Hole)?

WHEN we should be **INFORMED** - so we, at least, **KNOW where we are heading!**

Oh! For the love of CLARITY!

LEFT: HOW do we **secure the future for Everybody?**

RIGHT: We wont supply the DETAILS.

LEFT: Into this breach, we go:

CHAPTER 2

WHAT'S THE ANSWER?

THE FUTURE IS MODULAR

A GOOD PRODUCT - FOR THE SPACE AGE

THIS IS A *BASIC MODULE*

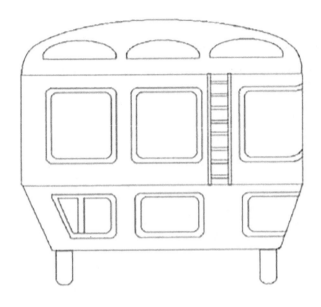

Cute is its middle name.
Just call me 'it' for short.

'it' stands for:

interlocking technology or, **intelligent thinking**
MODULAR
THE SENSIBLE WAY TO UPDATE!

it **PROVIDES ESSENTIAL ACCOMMODATION**
TO END THE HOUSING SHORTAGE,
AND RELIEVE POVERTY!

PREFABRICATED (some Advantages)

- Manufactured indoors - unaffected by weather
- Professionally assembled
- Pre-agreed, fixed, LOWER COST/S
- Quick delivery
- Reduced waiting times, less stress...

"it is **BETTER BY DESIGN**"

SUPER-STRONG: Modern materials and techniques **SUPERCEDE** existing **LOW** standards **OUT-PERFORMING** conventional builds with enhanced longevity.

A **VARIETY** of shapes and styles are possible. The basic Module is easy to **ADAPT**, and **EXTEND** as needed.

it is **VERSATILE**
Modules (or, Crafts) are a new-style of HOUSING**S**
to make **SHELTERS** (and **VEHICLES** for transport).

STACK & STORE (it's made in two halves?)

Carefully stack the manufactured Casings (or Shells) and store those ready to be interlocked / assembled.

LIGHTWEIGHT (no heavy chassis...) so easy to mobilise.

Governments should have a **READY-MADE SUPPLY OF MODULES** - in a depot, or wherever... a (Safe) Stockpile available for Emergency **LOCAL distribution**, to provide assistance when shelters are required **QUICKLY**, for the **HEALTH & SAFETY OF CITIZENS.**

**USE THIS BASIC MODULE TO REDUCE
SOCIAL SUFFERING,
STRAINS & BURDENS!**

GIVE A BASIC MODULE / EMERGENCY SHELTER that functions as a *NEW DECENT STARTER HOME,* to each adult person, or family surviving a disaster.

MEET NEEDS! The required **HUMANE** response.

Is it too much to ask for, and expect?

SAFE, CLEAN, COMFORT. That matters to all of us.

On this, I hope we AGREE? YES / NO

A decent roof over people's heads keeping them SAFE, dry and warm - but not too hot - is important.
Able to manage happily, and well.
Each person has what they need to flourish.
That makes **GOOD SENSE**.

There is no justifiable excuse not *to do it.*

NO **Arguments,** ifs, or buts *PLEASE.*

You just need to be KIND, be considerate towards others,
have some *COMPASSION - to UNDERSTAND.*

A FAIR DEAL, DELIVERED.

That is the way forward.

TO **PROVIDE PROTECTION**
THESE MODULES ARE
A **BASIC NECESSITY**

YES, it IS A...
LIFE SUPPORT SYSTEM
HERE TO HELP YOU!

it **IS <u>WEATHER-PROOF</u>**

Water does not harm or penetrate it because it is made from **Water <u>RESISTANT</u>** material, and its joints are **<u>WATER TIGHT</u>**.

On water, *it* **FLOATS...**

VERY IMPORTANT! NO LEAKS!

(Underwater cameras with seamless casings wouldn't be great if water got in).
No skimping now - *it's* a very basic Must-Have!

its **<u>DOUBLE HULL</u>** provides **EXCELLENT INSULATION** (same principle as a thermos flask). The space between casings - the cavity - is filled with water (stored in a strong blue hose?)

WATER ADDS WEIGHT *(to stop it toppling over...)*
it is **Heavier** at the bottom...

it **<u>COLLECTS RAINWATER</u>** via a drainage system on the roof – rain is gravity fed (water is not stored on the roof), and it **RECYCLES** water...

SEWAGE is collected – that is "rich organic matter" (in a strong, wide, flat, heavier red hose – put under the raised modular ground floor?) Non-smelly, **dried pellets** are used to speed the growth of Trees...

"... and when the **shit** hits the fan?" Minor problems we can sort out. What we can't do is carry on **deferring problems!**

INSPECTION PANEL

Easy-Access, with a pump? Gauge, and Connector (to resupply the system from elsewhere if there has been insufficient rainfall), plus a Fill / Empty switch, & Filter with Tests - to check water Quality.

SAFE, CLEAN POWER:

For lights, fridge, cooking, gadgets...

its **ENERGY** (for now) could be supplied by:

A WISE COMBINATION OF RENEWABLES:

- Silent, mini wind turbine/s (horizontal)
- Industrial-strength Solar cells (use day-light)
- Hydro – such as mini water wheels
- Kinetic
- Some Human power (dynamo fitness equipment)

SURPLUS / ENERGY STORAGE

MINIATURISED batteries / **PORTABLE** Power Pack/s

Recharges via the Mains supply should not be necessary. Many devices could supply the grid without risk or outages.

"... companies needing to **REINVEST** could make the **LOW-COST equipment** needed - there is plenty of profit in that."

Fitments improved later by occupants...

Other ideas when researching, for easing
THE ENERGY CRISIS – so customers have *GREATLY REDUCED* **BILLS,** and we have **SAFE, steady PROGRESS:**

A. Water companies could install mini water wheels in pressurised Mains water supply pipes...
B. Use microwave technology (not gas) for domestic heating...
C. *Please properly Redesign the Alternator:*
AS WE TRAVEL: Capture Energy: From the movement of wheels on vehicles... And, via the movement of air: Fit specially-made, small, flat Wind turbine/s on vehicles – on roofs... (And put in the wind-tunnels between buildings...)

SIZE OF Basic Module

Same as a bus? Minus the section for the driver?
Yes, 2 storeys! A double-decker. *Why not?*
We are all individuals – some tall, some in wheel-chairs... tailor *it to fit...*

WHAT'S THE BEST MATERIAL *to make it with?*

Plastic is such a fantastic, useful material. (Where would modern Healthcare be without it?)
We grew up having been told plastic is "**Disposable**." (To sell more, I don't doubt).

(Are Petro-chemical companies getting away with the costs of **repairing** the **damages DRILLING & wrongful dumping** has done to the Environment?)

Every piece of plastic should be appreciated & valued, not tossed thoughtlessly away as "rubbish"!
Say NO to SHORT-Life!

All the **WATER-RESIST, NON-BIODEGRADEABLE** plastic that's already been made should be recycled and sensibly refashioned – preserving it to make life *easier* for New Generations.

(INTELLIGENT WASTE DISPOSAL = Do not make, use or buy anything that **cannot** be recycled).

SNEER: "Is it a **PLASTIC** house?"

The current trend is to make houses from recycled plastic bottles etc., derived from (Fossil Fuel) oil.

H'mm. "Anything made from oil **burns**... Additives are..."

The material it should be made from is not soft, squishy, or brittle - it is **RIGID,** UV stabilised, and
Able to Withstand Extremes of Temperature...

I know it's going to make you laugh...

it is not something to be sneered at.

NOTE:

In the **COMMERCIAL** world, it is up to **END-USER/S** to **SPECIFY** their desired performance. The manufacturer then comes up with a suitable product to satisfy.

(That is great especially when backed up with a *Life?* **LONG GUARANTEE** that is honoured, in the unlikely event their product is not as sold).

WE SHOULD AIM FOR:
THE BEST QUALITY POSSIBLE!

LONG LIFE: OUR GOAL: A (cold set?) material that ensures Maximum Resilience and *ultimate* **DURABILITY**, derived from an Eco-Friendly, pleasant-smelling process - a Non-Hazardous, inflammable, *CLEAR SOLUTION*.

RESIN: (Look at Amber – that is a form of natural resin - it really is very beautiful).

Is it made from Resin?
Derived from a bio oil that's not **BIODEGRADABLE?** Really!? Hemp Oil?

GROWING ORGANIC HEMP is Green and **GOOD FOR THE ENVIRONMENT** "... it efficiently removes carbon from the atmosphere..." "...All the derivatives of hemp could provide an **ENTIRE NEW ECONOMY**, offering *SUSTAINABLE* growth..."

Resin could also be made from (abundant) sand (silicon) found in deserts with factories powered entirely by solar, using robots.

"WITH CHEMISTRY, *ANYTHING IS POSSIBLE."*
it's like baking a cake and changing the ingredients...
You just need to know the correct recipe.

END USERS LIKE PRECISION MADE!

Make Super-Strong LIGHT-weight Modules using CAD/ CAM etc., in factories...

HELP STRENGTHEN LOCAL COMMUNITIES by *SHARING* moulds, know-how etc.

it creates NEW GOOD JOBS!

HOW TO PUT *it* TOGETHER?

What *JOINT* technique allows *it* to be securely put together, and disassembled? *CLICK. And it's fixed.*

MAKE it in any **COLOUR / PATTERN** imaginable - *it could be made to resemble* quaint Old-style wood, Mother-of-Pearl... Make it holographic, glittery?

(Are you scared of *colour?* Every UK caravan by law, has to be white, to remind us of fridges? Or sludge green, or beige? Yuk).

it has a **ONE-PIECE**, snap-on **ROOF**
(like a Tupperware lid) (additionally secured from the *inside...*)

its roof has (pre-fitted / moulded-in) *SOLAR* **DOMES**
(Opaque for privacy...)

"I want to enjoy living seeing the bright Starlight..."

A central, circular, hollow, **STRENGTHENING CORE**

- could have a large/r domed Light-inlet
- the interior of the Core lined with angled mirrors - plus a magnifier, to Amplify light / protons?

- an inner core could rotate? (and be attached to...)
- the space inside the Core could be serviced by a little robot
- fit a console around the outside of the Core to mini-mise wiring, and securely store devices there

TO CREATE ROOM/S / FLEXIBLE PARTITIONING

Arrange in a star shape - around the outer Core =
every room has a window...

NO CUTS! NO JAGGED SHARDS!

WINDOWS

- High-strength / _deter_ **Crime** / robbers...
- Coo! Curved (like windscreens) panoramic windows...
- its smaller windows open manually _and_ electroni-cally (see: cool classic cars designs)
- Airplane windows have a handy built-in shutter... (No, it isn't going to be curtains for all of us!)
- Install wipers on _all its windows?_

its Main **DOORS** slide open sideways (see: Tube trains).
Push-button (operated by air pressure?) Ultimately, _when you go inside it, you could enter an Airlock._

it's **A STEP UP**

DUAL-USE: Steps could convert into a non-slip *RAMP, that is also a draw-bridge / extra shutter* - by flicking a switch.

Adding a pneumatic *LIFT using a strong transparent (resin) tube* is not inconceivable...

A re/moveable **LADDER** runs on a *(non-metal)* rail around the outside of the Module...

Yes, it is **HYGENIC.** Wash it with a hose. Yes, it only needs a quick wash to stay *EVER-BRIGHT - all Twinkly!*

"... it makes a refreshing change from strange bed-fellows!" No unwanted bugs! If **Germs** are a problem, *it is ideal for safe* **Quarantine**, to reduce and avoid contamination.

it is an Equipped Tech-**LOGICAL**, No-Perish, new **PREFAB** - made possible, with thanks to **MODERN TECHNOLOGY.**

HOW it SHOULD BE DONE:

FOR SECURITY: *it is ESSENTIAL KIT!*

it is **NON-HARMFUL.** *There is nothing to fear about it – it is not dangerous* - prototypes will have been **FULLY TESTED** - all Risks expertly (and conscientiously) erradicated.

it is a **LOW-COST,** *SAFE HOME for those who need it* because they have **not** got one.

GOVERNMENT HELP

By using their <u>purchase power</u> to lower costs via **BULK ORDERS**, and helping citizens by offering them 0% **INTEREST-FREE**, Flexible purchase plans...

GOVERNMENTS ACTIVELY ENCOURAGE

COST-EFFECTIVE MODULES BECAUSE:

- Modules MINIMISE the costs of disasters
- SAVE time, money and LIVES
- Assist & promote HEALTH & Safety
- Help the Environment and the Economy
- Improve the Quality of Life
- Significantly reduce burdens - with little or no long-term dependence on taxpayers' money

Modules are a great way to save the Public Purse.

For example: Modules should be used to provide _NEW HOMES_ for _CARE IN THE COMMUNITY,_ to lower Social Care bills (free-ing hospital beds...)

HAVE YOU GOT YOUR HEAD AROUND it YET?

it is a LIGHT craft, it is there in an instant, everything is on board to make life as PLEASANT as possible.

it resists floods, it does not burn, it is not explosive or polluting.

it is not made of timber or metal, it does not rot or fall to bits, it is maintenance free.

it feels smooth, it looks WONDERFUL, it simply does the job for a very long time. Then it is FULLY RECYCLABLE.

Yes, people live and work in it - it is a new **HOME OFFICE**... _with it,_ there won't be **Hard Knocks...**

it's **NEEDED AS IF THERE IS NO TOMORROW...**

Oh! it is such a RELIEF!

TO SITE *it*

Put it almost anywhere
(though I wouldn't risk my home near a volcano).

- **TEMPORARY SITE:** *Free-stand it.* **No concrete / foundation necessary.** Built-in LEGS *raise it off* the ground (like a Pilotis)
- Adjust each leg to level it on **UNEVEN GROUND** by using a simple lever
- Ski's and wide "feet" can be put on the base of its legs...
- **TO INCREASE** it's **HEIGHT:** Extend each (tele-scopic) leg adding another section - its legs could also be Retractable and Hydraulic...
- it's **SEMI / PERMANENT:** Slot / couple its legs into strong,hollow posts / rigid tubes, secured into the ground - quickly and effortlessly auto / releasing the Module as necessary
- Hint: Using cranes to lift *it* should not be necessary

WELCOME TO _BRILLSVILLE!_

There are plenty of places where it can be put.

Just slot it in!

Yes, it fills gaps _BEAUTIFULLY!_

- it is _SELF-SUFFICIENT- it fully functions on its own_
- it does **not** need to be attached to Mains services
- it saves the cost of installing underground pipes, overhead cables...
- _it is ideal in remote areas to sustain life_

There is plenty of **LAND** Available.

See: **ALL THE IDLE, UNPRODUCTIVE, LONELY** Fields?

IMAGINE meadows full of wild flowers with TREES, clean, sweet air, and a few Modules, dotted about like sheep on a hillside...

What better way is there to enjoy SPACE?

<u>Just think about it</u>.

<u>MODULE PARKS</u>

INTRODUCE new, **<u>well-managed</u>** Module parks, in many places around the world, to provide a thriving global community linked via modern communications - people sharing knowledge and skills - making things to benefit local areas and countries...

Each park fully functioning and **ENJOYING** housing with **GREATLY** <u>**REDUCED RUNNING COSTS**</u>.

Module parks open to join, and people visit - selecting according to their preferences, and the interests at the parks that are catered for... Some could also provide shelter for animals... The cows can come home!

MODULAR LIVING!

Some support holidays, week-end retreats... for non-residents to sample *what it's like...*

GROW HEALTHY FOOD <u>LOCALLY!</u>

IMAGINE **SENIOR CITIZENS** blissfully pottering about helping bees... advising and showing younger people how to grow their own healthy food (without using insecticides and chemical weedkillers).

Don't worry! You'll still get your cornflakes...

GROW FOOD INSIDE MODULES!
Yes, grow plants / food *inside it...*

<u>it is FUN!</u>

I would love to see _contented_ kids in _MODULAR_ classrooms each designing their own ideal Modular home - learning how to do it - motivated by the reassurance - you will _definitely get it, and benefit from it._

REALISING DREAMS – it matters!

it is HASSLE-FREE LIVING!

Ooh! Lots of lovely Brillsvilles everywhere scattered all over the world... lots of Eco-projects, HELPING nature, and conservation...

I strongly believe we should be allowed to:

INTEGRATE _it,_ to Transform lives...

No, we don't want the country-side **choked** with tons of cars!

But we can still make use of existing (pot-holed) roads and transport until manufacturers _get it together..._

GROAN: Until then, add tyres?

Or push it?

DO YOU ENJOY JOINING VERY LARGE DOTS?

Picture the ultimate model...
MAKE MODULES MOBILE!

To start off with, just a controllable safe rise up - at least a few inches off the ground. *HOVER without* choppers / blades, jet fuel, blast, or rubber skirt.
(Yes, you do need to get to the bottom of it...)

G'WHIZZ!

When it travels, it doesn't carry **heavy flammable fuel** *- it is* LIGHT *weight, CLEAN, SAFE, truly delightful - it goes with* *no* **flash, big noise, bang, or smoke...**

I know I need one! I like handy dinky-dos.
See you in a jiffy! A little quick hover is no bother.
Don't want to be late, *do we?*

Embed... LIGHT cells... Plenty of renewable SAFE *(non-***explosive***) energy (NO* **hazardous waste***)...*

When we understand this *simple concept...* *it starts to become an IDENTIFIED object...*

... not **disturbing** *the PEACE OF THE UNIVERSE!*

Are we all doing a great big **TIME-AND-MOTION** study?

So we learn _BETTER WAYS_.

That seems to beckoning to us: _Come on! Understand it_!

The TASK Ahead for Mankind?

Just IMPLEMENT it.

CHAPTER 3

THE CHRONIC HOUSING SHORTAGE

In the UK, many people unable to afford mortgage repayments are **trapped** in **unsuitable** rented property and are also unable to pay rent. (**TAXPAYERS** have the burden of paying <u>**UNAFFORDABLE**</u> **RENTS** via the government's **£HUGE Annual bill**).

I wonder how many of those people would relish the opportunity to <u>escape</u> the **OVER-CROWDED** 'Population Centres' / Cities, *to enjoy something different?*

OUTMODED LEGAL RESTRICTIONS assisting **PROFITEERS** and racketeers are not helping to *ease* "life" for the majority...

Trying to get and keep a roof over your head – so you <u>have some feeling of security</u>, is dreadfully **HARD AND DIFFICULT** these days. Years go by in the **maze**, and you're still not winning **"THE HOUSING LOTTERY..."**

Anxiety and depression kicks in...

Why don't governments do *something* **PRACTICAL** to help relieve this **CRIPPLING** bottle-neck?

Take some **PRESSURE** off!

MAKE THE PROCESS SIMPLE!

IF politicians genuinely care, they'd **DO** *it* just to help **MENTAL** *HEALTH!*

PATIENT No. 95789567: "I can't sleep, I can't put my finger on it, but I'm tired of the same old.."

PSYCHIATRIST: **"It's all in your head."**

PATIENT: **"Nothing external** is considered by you! *That's* the problem. **Don't** you know **What's Going On**? Don't **FORCE** me to take more potions and pills! I don't need those..."

Oh! For the *LOVE* of a *conducive place...*

IMPRISONING / PERVERTING / CRIMINALISING...
Is it not better?

it **IS ESPECIALLY** <u>**VITAL**</u> **TO** <u>**HELP**</u>

The people (of All Ages) desirous of <u>LEAFY surrounds</u>
and <u>The YOUNG</u>
because New Generation/s are very sadly
PRICED OUT OF THE PROPERTY MARKET.

Where are they supposed to live??

MANY PEOPLE ARE HOMELESS:
That means: "<u>Without</u> a place to live."

Leaving Citizens to **DIE** on the streets, and locking the homeless out-of-sight in **PRISONS** is **not** the answer.

Build more prisons rather than solve anything?

Don't you want to assist people worse off than you?

GOD **SAVE THE PEOPLE!**

EXCLUDED, and trying to live *OFF-GRID...*

Many people are trying to sleep in cars, vans, caravans, trailers... None of those are well-insulated.

ALL THE STRUGGLES just to keep warm, or cool enough!

"We can't run the engine to keep warm or the battery dies..."
"Sweltering! We can't afford to run the air conditioning..."
"... so **difficult** to have a shower..."

WISHING every day for *SELF-SUFFICIENCY...*

Thinking-up / inventing / working out **LOW-TECH** ways to make **LOW COST** devices to make lives just a bit *easier...*

Politicians cruelly joke about the "unwashed" oblivious to the efforts made by <u>worthy</u> people who are just trying their best to cope, too often in harsh and gruelling conditions – usually due to cicumstances beyond their control.

"There is always *something* to hope for."

HOPE is what many people are running on!

I don't know where your happy place is, but governments are **DELUDED** if they think those who are really suffering do not want *something better.*

NEEDED:

Practical / good / *<u>STATE-OF-THE-ART</u>*

<u>WEATHER-PROOF EMERGENCY SHELTERS</u>:

In the UK, the most people get for flood "relief" is **sand** (that may be shovelled into sacks or plastic bags for you).

When fouled water breaches **sandbag barriers** / **INADEQUATE** *DEFENCES* – gushing into buildings **RUINING** everything worked hard for, a school Hall (or similar) is opened (by the council, or kind volunteers) so **traumatised EVACUATED victims** can doss on a floor, or camp bed surrounded by strangers...

Houses take ages to dry out... After previous floods, can't get insurance... Premiums go up...

"What if the Hall is under water?"

"...obviously alternate accommodation is needed..."

AT LEAST HALF THE WORLD'S POPULATION IS STARVING & SUFFERING BAD HOUSING, POVERTY, AND SQUALOR

OVERSEAS "AID": <u>Not Uncommon Sights to See</u>:

Unclothed, starving, badly dehydrated children scrambling on their knees in dust to get a few grains of uncooked rice dropped by well-fed soldiers...

Tents & heavy military Aid <u>TAKES AGES to arrive</u> (often flown and shipped in from abroad!) whilst the painfully ravaged poor survivors of gut-wrenching disasters wait outside (even in snow!) **wet, freezing, hungry, thirsty, exhausted, desperate...**

"WAH! I feel so INSECURE."

They fled their homes to save their lives, only to end up stuck indefinitely in a city of canvas tents plonked on a sea of mud... gaping flapping holes partially covered with tatty, _LIFE-SAVING_ bits of plastic...

Inside each tent too many despondent, desperate, frightened people just trying somehow! to survive...
sub-existing MISERABLY...

DAMAGE ASSESSMENT

How many people **DIED** in those tents?
Did anyone bother to count?

Yes, a tent is "better than nothing." **BUT**

PL-EASE IMPROVE HOW WE **"RESCUE" PEOPLE!**

"DO NOT FORGET SCOTT OF THE ANTARTIC!"

It is not possible to better yourself when you are battling against "bad" weather, in a very poor shelter, lacking provisions...

GLOBAL WARMING
The Earth's **CLIMATE IS** *CHANGING!*

THE SERIOUS THREATS OF: Rising sea levels, increased flooding, land loss, more storms, freak weather, very hot temperatures / desertification, followed by a new **Ice Age.**

To add to our **DISCOMFORT** the very **REAL RISK** of **POWER OUTAGES** in winter etc., because National Grids / pylons etc., **can't** cope, and give up the ghost.

The **ADVERSE EFFECTS...** A likely **SCENARIO?**

Yet more disasters, such as many towns flooded by over-flowing rivers, towns washed away…

Many more people **HOMELESS...**

The **MAYHEM could be... OVERWHELMING?**

POLLUTION from Burning Oil...
HEATING our Atmosphere...
DROUGHTS... houses in **flames,** forest **fires**
(with helicopters trying to douse - using **heavy water,** not foam...)

That is all going to be **VERY COSTLY.**

There's not enough water - there's too much water – we are surrounded by salty water we **can't** drink – because governments have **FAILED** to ensure *adequate investment in... DESALINATION plants...*

<u>THERE IS NO</u> *CIVIL DEFENCE PLAN!*

WE ARE <u>UNPREPARED!</u>

SITTING DUCK SYNDROME
(this is one label psychiatrists haven't used yet):

We know **CLIMATE CHANGE** could affect us, but we hope we can get away with it! Everybody hopes the next bad storm does not hit them.

<u>We **haven't** a clue how we will cope if the worst happens.</u>

We feel sorry and grieve for the poor unfortunates - all those **WIPED OUT**... **"LIVING IN FEAR"** <u>we carry-on **CHANGING NOTHING**</u> that will make a difference.

We are tired of **HEAVY LOSSES** and all the heart-breaking TV adverts wanting us to donate more money to charities...

The entire Human population is **STUCK** in a **DEGENERATIVE** Loop! <u>**AT RISK.**</u>

The Whole World is WAITING and PRAYING for "*some-*

thing" **to Happen.** *WHAT??*

PROPERTY DEVELOPERS?

Do they only want more **COSTLY** brick houses (and tradition-
al-looking houses made from rendered ply) <u>requiring con-
nection to Mains services</u> – using **timber** and **heavy** transport (for mind boggling high numbers of pieces...) Painfully
SLOW, unmoveable "new" builds - that **DON'T** prevent
water flooding in, because that's where the money is?

All the **REBUILDING THE SAME WAY** after a storm has
reduced rows of **timber houses** to "matchsticks"!

<u>**NOT** *SUSTAINABLE*</u> - **MORE DEFORESTATION?**

We need <u>TREES / ENRICHED OXYGEN</u> (not **timber**) to
improve <u>AIR QUALITY</u>, so we can breathe...

"WHAT ABOUT THE THREAT TO <u>PUBLIC SAFETY</u>?"

We are going to have to rely on **Antiquated** Builds?
We are not in the 1800s!

FOR PUBLIC RELATIONS: "STICK TO THE SCRIPT"

"There is **no** alternative. We **are** doing everything we can. We need **concrete**... It's **not** in the public interest..."

That is <u>MISINFORMATION</u>. Who is OK with that?

GOVERNMENTS REFUSING to put in place the help needed to adequately *PROTECT* people is really very **<u>WORRYING</u>**. Their job is to keep **THE PEOPLE** *<u>SAFE!</u>*

In the meantime, remember we **HEAVILY DEPEND** on **(imported) <u>FOOD</u>** supplies etc., transported by ships, airplanes, lorries... using **COMBUSTION** engines **BURNING** oil - **<u>WHEN</u>** we really should be *REDUCING* **CARBON EMISSIONS**.

<u>If it's not produced,</u> *HOW ARE WE GOING TO SWITCH* **from FOSSIL FUELS?**

Does the British government seriously believe building a few more terribly expensive Nuclear stations to generate power <u>for a few thousand homes</u>... backing giant turbines to power the aged grid, **(<u>Explosive</u>)** <u>Hydrogen</u>... and very expensive "self-charging" hybrid electric cars (only the rich can afford to buy to save money - that most people can't afford to buy)...is going to **SAVE US** from the effects of **CLIMATE CHANGE?**

DOES THE WORLD WANT *kind, considerate, caring, <u>COMPASSIONATE</u> changes to be made QUICKLY?*

WHAT MAKE US UNHEALTHY AND UNHAPPY?
NOT having what we need.
Yes, talk about Security - *the options...*

"I'm OK. I don't need it."
Great. But other people do - it's a step up for them that you could ramp up...

"I still don't see the need for it."

Whilst you are deciding which camp you are in...

UNITING US

The **HUMAN RIGHT** to have a **HOME**...
The same problems affect every country.
We are all under the weather.
We are all vulnerable.
"Life on Earth depends on the Climate..."

Within Human Beings there is a courageous striving for Peace, Stability, and Prosperity...

We, the *GOOD* people of Earth (hopefully) UNITED, need to **WAKE-UP GOVERNMENTS** who should not be encouraging all Citizens to be "**CONSUMERS**" **ravaging** the Planet - to prop-up declining Economies (based on Fossil fuels).

That throws the baby out with the bathwater!

WISE-UP!

HALF of the World's Population is a HUGE MARKET, and *its VAST POTENTIAL* is currently untapped.

If Governments truly want *SUSTAINABLE, Economic progression, they should help Develop it!*

DON'T FORGET: There is no other **LOW-COST** / truly affordable / pollution-free option available.

No politician/s or vehicle manufacturer/s have come up with ideas for anything to replace the sort of (tin) vehicles still favoured! And the transportation that is mass-produced, is **NOT** *WATER TIGHT.*

Is the **LACK** of *water-tight housings* starting to bother you? "Water-tight" is another word rarely mentioned by the media even when reporting the tragic loss of many lives when an airplane went down over the sea, and sank.

OPEN TOP, rusting SHIPS...
Giant Waves swamping...
"Oh, the bilge pump doesn't work!"

Why on Earth are there so many **BAD** *designs?*

Yes, to survive, "we must **ADAPT**." *HOW??*

Put a lid on "The Tupperware fleet"?

FAILURE to *sort it out* could mean

The **EXTINCTION** of *HUMAN BEINGS.*

its potential to help HUMANITY must not be **sabotaged** by **greedy, selfish Exploiters!**

*For example: it **only** gets made into a **LUXURY** item to **compete** with **Glass**-fibre yachts!*

That would be a **CRIME AGAINST HUMANITY!**

MAKING it should be **PRIORITY NUMBER ONE** in every country via international collaboration - so every aspect is correctly resourced, developed, & progressed.

ASSIGN A SPECIAL TEAM (via the UN)

CHEMISTS, ENGINEERS, architects, and others... *it is a puzzle of only a few pieces... it must work...*

Make it snappy! Do it NOW before it is **TOO LATE!**

I don't know how else to tell you what you probably already know.

it IS A... NEW DECENT STARTER HOME
a SAFE, clean, HAPPY, Healthy GOOD Home...

Year 3000

it MADE THINGS BETTER - HEALTHY AND HAPPY: Just try to imagine - see in your mind what life could look like then. *Can you see it? Is it a much nicer future?*
Think about that.

I hope shaping the future matters as much to YOU as much as *it does to me.* I don't want to see **vast buildings made using tons of crude metal Meccano-sets, cruel masters, slaves forced to pay-for-Oxygen, nothing else is living** (if I am reincarnated and forced to come back here!)

Don't listen to **WAR MONGERERS** who say:
"Strap that **bomb** to your body - that's the only way to 'paradise'." Believe me: *The opposite is required* to **MORE BLOODy SHED/s**!

With it, we EVOLVE. We find we don't have to **misuse** and **hurt** others, **DESTROY**, or **mine** natural worlds **spreading death and destruction**.

WE ARE ABLE to follow a PEACEFUL path, NURTURING and Valuing LIFE.

We stop **wasting, disrespecting, misspending**, and **squandering** wealth on **things** we don't really need...

... such as **OVERPOWERFUL** cars...

**Do you have more MONEY
than you *KNOW* what to do with?**

INVESTOR: "How much does it cost to make one?"

"Pennies compared to the many $**TRILLIONS WASTED** on very silly things."

it's A...
GREEN MODULE:

CHALLENGE:

PRODUCE *this little one!*
Yes, work it out – including its component parts.

*Do that, believe it or not, and you will really help
to* <u>RESCUE</u> *this planet, and its people.*

Ah! for a Fun life!

Deserts *GREENED...*

Year 2000

This is supposed to be:
"...a time of <u>HAPPY</u> government..."

Londoners with no choice celebrated the arrival of a giant **TENT**! (Cost to make the Millennium Dome £800 million).

its Momentous Millennial <u>APPEARANCE</u>
was an **<u>OPPORTUNITY MISSED</u>**!

One day, Earth's leaders might **OPENLY <u>DISCUSS</u>** *it?*

Are they going to talk... and talk...
at Conventions **until HELL FREEZES OVER?**

it's very sad. Because they need *it* too!

> *"Some will take an eternity to believe*
> *it lends itself to everything."*

My advice is don't wait on them, or hang around.

WHERE IS *it?*

WAH! *The Marvellous Module is* **NOWHERE** to be found!

"It's a fairy tale, right?" *ABSOLUTELY NOT!*
"Can you think about it for more than 10 seconds?"
"I won't believe it until I see it." "Seeing is believing."
Ah! ye of little faith!
Demonstrate it?

But it is up to you what you do with your time.

JOIN *the Human* <u>*RACE*</u>: <u>*it needs Your Help*</u>:

IF *you want* *it to be done - on Earth*
(because you believe *it is a good thing to do),*
the dawn chorus to this bird's song?
Well, it goes something like this:

Flippin' hell,
it makes sense!
Let's get on wth it!

Are we going to live happily ever after?
HOPEFULLY!

GOOD LUCK!
Ah! **that means** <u>*you are going to need it*</u>.

ALONE IN A QUIET ROOM

3am. Light on - *it's all good – quiet...*

Awake. **Pondering:**

"Life" is a TEST? <u>To find out if our spirit is good, or bad.</u>
Money is the tool used to tempt some people... to **Evil.**
Money should be used to help people.
It's only kind people that make life worth living.
Hoarding - money surely is an **ILLNESS**.

What is the point of life if we don't *do something wonderful?*
If we take, take, take - give nothing back? If we don't use our
time wisely making life *EASIER?*

These days, too many choices!? Confusing. How to decide
what is best for you? Are we between the devil and the deep
sea? Accept what is – conform - sell your soul, if necessary? Or, look after mind and spirit believing in freedom from
tyranny even that kills you? Do what you think you "have to"
to survive?

WHAT ABOUT *THE FEEL GOOD FACTOR?*

How to fill days to _FEEL GOOD?_ (I don't mean "drowning" - worries / problems - bothering / eating away at you, get drunk for a fake euphoria followed by sickness!)

True contentment is being sure you're in the clear and on top of things so you feel at _PEACE,_ high on fresh air, able to breathe deeply. Do most people have that satisfied **STRESS**-free feeling today?

THE COLLECTIVE CONCIOUS?

It's not bad to wish things are _easier._ I'm not the only one wishing - so it would be good for progress to work collectively together to _IMPROVE THINGS_ – starting that conversation – _it's very much about HEALING_... so others don't suffer unnecessarily / painfully – using our minds, abilities, time and resources to really achieve _making life easier,_ so it gets easier to be Human.

What is Human? Being intelligent and capable of understanding & feeling _COMPASSION._ Many animals have that inborn intelligence... so a clearer definition would help.

Some humans think **it's wrong** to care? - that they are "better off" pretending not to, because caring is **too painful?** caring only causes **conflict/s**? More convenient? to go along with what-is? than walk away from what they know is bad!

But in our hearts surely we know it's correct to <u>CARE</u>. I'm not ashamed to admit I CARE, a lot!

<u>The **WAR** between those with *EMPATHY* and Sociopathic narcissists – the perpretrators of abuse & aggression</u>...

Difficult to know who is what inside as we all look similar.

The empathy gene is missing in some people's DNA - a rare few? in serial killers, psychopaths - not all – only some. <u>Therefore 99.9% of Humans feel *COMPASSION*!?</u>

SO it's FAR FROM A HOPELESS STRUGGLE!

(Yes, it's buried more deeply in some whilst for others it's a strong part of their nature).

But we hear about "Humans" causing the worst pits of depravity! That pit is a place in the minds of Humans yes, but <u>most of us</u> don't even want to take a small step towards that – we do everything possble to avoid – "don't go there!" because self-destructive irrational mania is far from normal behaviour, even when severely prevoked or triggered – and even then, in that rare event, freedom from pain and torment is desperately sought. I think that's our saving grace.

Humans can make bad mistakes but <u>most of us</u> reflect on the consequences (of anger...) the damages... and need to appease – desiring to go back in time if we could to undo injuries – even taking away all the pain of others.

Yes, there are people who act mean and nasty – who take our breath away sometimes with the sheer scale of their audacity. But even they can stop, and use *COMPASSION*, albeit at a slow pace.

COMMON SENSE *PREVAILS!*

Of course it would be easier to be a Human
if we all just **"DO-AS-YOU-WOULD-BE-DONE-BY."**

Unfortunately some Humans don't adhere to that principle – they enjoy? causing tortuous torment on others robotically. But, note, when the tables are turned – their turn now to be hurt, they blub for forgiveness, beg, and plead for *COMPASSION to be shown* to them.

FURTHER INFORMATION

"There's a lot more to it."

I can't describe everything quintessential here as I have to keep this short to be practical.

FULL OF FACTS

A copy of my extensive research (compiled) Information directory will hopefully be made available & printed on _LIGHT_ weight paper, IF / when a publisher agrees there is sufficient interest in *it*.

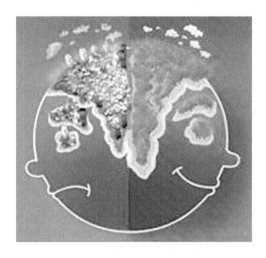

DISCLAIMER

This entirely **INDEPENDENT critical review** - not affiliated to any business, political party or religious group, is presented under the provisions of Fair Use for Social, economic and Environmental reasons, to help *ADVANCE HUMANITY.*

Printed in Great Britain
by Amazon

77954017R00047